■■SCHOLASTIC

Grades
3-4

TIC-TAC-MATH

**50 Reproducible, Leveled Game Sheets That Kids
Can Use Independently or in Small Groups
to Practice Important Math Skills**

by Matt Friedman

NEW YORK • TORONTO • LONDON • AUCKLAND • SYDNEY
MEXICO CITY • NEW DELHI • HONG KONG • BUENOS AIRES

Teaching *Resources*

To Laura and Lilly—
for loving all of my pluses and minuses

Cover design by Jaime Lucero
Interior design by Grafica, Inc.
Illustrations by Doug Jones

ISBN 0-439-62920-9
Copyright © 2005 by Matt Friedman
All rights reserved.
Printed in the U.S.A.

1 2 3 4 5 6 7 8 9 10   40   12 11 10 09 08 07 06 05

Table of Contents

Table of Contents

Introduction

Welcome to *Tic-Tac-Math: Grades 3–4!*
Your students are about to experience a wonderfully
educational twist on one of the most popular games of
all time. After all, what better way to grab students'
interest than to announce, "Today, we're going to play
a game!"

Just like classic tic-tac-toe, *Tic-Tac-Math* is played on
a three-by-three grid that students mark with X's and
O's to make a win. But unlike the traditional game, each square in the grid contains a
math problem that students have to solve correctly before they can claim the square with
their X or O.

What's Inside

Inside this book, you'll find 50 *Tic-Tac-Math* grids. Each grid covers a specific math skill
that is tied to at least one of the NCTM (National Council for Teachers of Mathematics)
standards. There are four sections that address the main standards: Number &
Operations, Measurement, Geometry, and Data Analysis & Probability.

The problems within each grid are leveled so that problems on the top row are
fairly easy, while the ones on the bottom row pose more of a challenge. For example, the
top row of an addition activity requires students to add two 2-digit numbers with no
regrouping. But by the bottom row, students are expected to add three 2-digit numbers
with multiple regroupings. Since the problems are leveled, you can decide which row (or
column or diagonal, if you want students to try a variety of difficulty levels) will benefit
each student the most. This way, every student can be working on the same topic but at
his or her own level. (Make photocopies of the blank grid on page 8 to use as answer
sheets for students or to create your own Tic-Tac-Math problems.)

Keep in mind that the point of each game is for students to practice and succeed at
that particular math skill. By the time students have completed every grid in the book, they
will have reviewed most of the math skills covered in grades 3 and 4. With those skills
under their command, students will feel confident with the problems presented on
standardized tests.

How to Use This Book

Tic-Tac-Math is a great way to reinforce a current math lesson or review a topic. Since each page focuses on a particular math topic, simply photocopy the page that corresponds with your unit of study and distribute to students.

Students can play *Tic-Tac-Math* with a partner, in small groups, or individually. Partners can play following the conventional rules of the game. Consider these additional rules as well:

- Flip a coin to decide who goes first, and who will be X and who will be O.

- If a player solves a problem correctly, that player marks the space with his or her letter (X or O).

- If the player answers incorrectly, the other player gets to mark that space with his or her letter *unless* that space would give the first player Tic-Tac-Math. (Players must correctly complete three problems in a row horizontally, vertically, or diagonally to get Tic-Tac-Math.)

- To win, a player must successfully solve the problem on the winning game space.

- Remind players to check each other's work!

Here are a few more ideas for using *Tic-Tac-Math:*

- **As a daily warm-up:** Have students complete three problems as a warm-up at the start of the class. Doing problems when students first enter the classroom helps them get settled and ready to work.

- **For "fast finishers":** Make sure to have some grids available to give students as a "What to Do When You're Done" activity.

- **For homework:** Send home a sheet for students to practice a particular skill. If you are working on adding fractions, for example, you can pass out a grid and assign students to complete any three problems—vertically, horizontally, or diagonally. Encourage students to play the game with parents or siblings.

- **As a choice activity:** Offer Tic-Tac-Math as a fun activity for choice time. Consider copying the grids onto cardstock and even laminating them so you can reuse them. Students can use different-colored counters instead of marking the grids with their X's and O's. Store the grids in a labeled folder or envelope for easy access. If you are using several different grids during one game session, encourage students to rotate around the room and play with as many other students as possible. Students gain a great deal from learning how to work with those to whom they might not normally gravitate toward in class.

Whichever approach you decide to use, your students are sure to enjoy themselves as they build the skills they need to succeed in math and on standardized tests. Let the games begin!

Name(s): _____

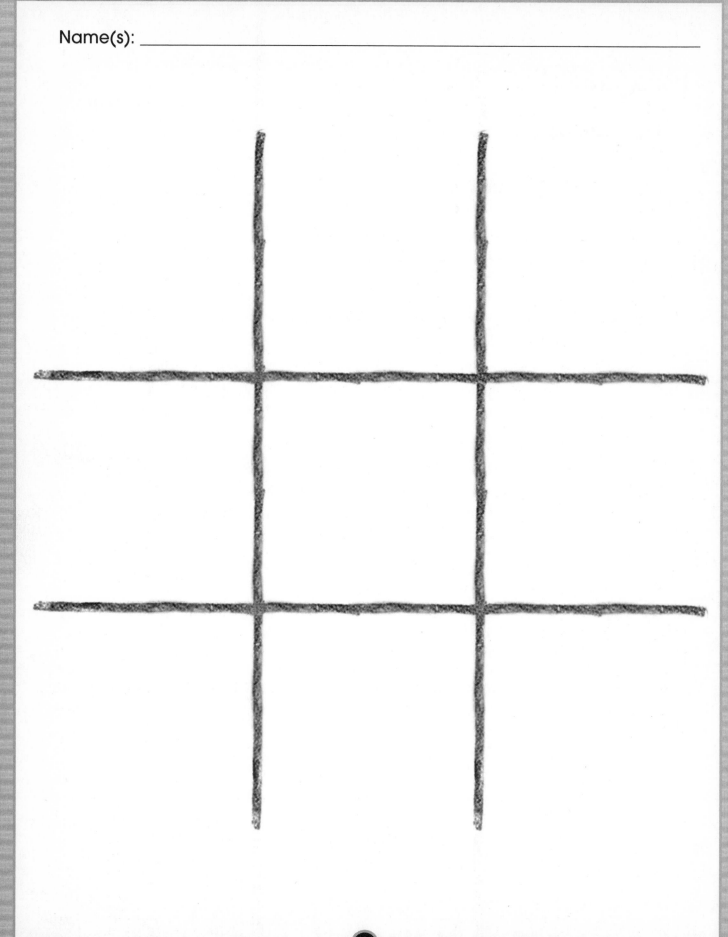

Name(s): _____

Order in the Court!

Now that we have your attention, put your skills at ordering numbers to the test. Solve three problems to get Tic-Tac-Math!

Fill in the box with >, <, or =.

27 ☐ 48

Fill in the box with >, <, or =.

298 ☐ 289

Fill in the box with >, <, or =.

731 ☐ 665

Fill in the box with >, <, or =.

4,256 ☐ 4,256

Fill in the box with >, <, or =.

58,132 ☐ 57,215

Fill in the box with >, <, or =.

72,340 ☐ 73,101

Order these numbers from least to greatest:

5,872
5,725
4,582
5,820

Order these numbers from least to greatest:

31,201
38,562
30,458
32,000
31,008

Order these numbers from least to greatest:

567,890
567,980
560,987
567,089
567,098

Scholastic • Tic-Tac-Math: Grades 3–4

Name(s): _____

The Rounding Hound

Help the rounding hound sniff out the right answers.
Solve three problems to get Tic-Tac-Math!

Round 82 to the nearest ten.	Round 36 to the nearest ten.	Round 65 to the nearest ten.
Round 439 to the nearest hundred.	Round 288 to the nearest hundred.	Round 749 to the nearest hundred.
Round 5,295 to the nearest thousand.	Round 87,401 to the nearest ten thousand.	Round 35,576 to the nearest ten.

Scholastic • Tic-Tac-Math: Grades 3–4

Name(s): _____

Do You See a Pattern?

I see several patterns here. Solve three pattern problems to get Tic-Tac-Math!

What's the next number in this pattern?

2, 4, 6, 8, _____

What's the next number in this pattern?

1, 4, 7, 10, _____

What's the next number in this pattern?

45, 40, 35, 30, _____

What are the next three numbers in this pattern?

18, 21, 20, 23, 22

_____, _____, _____

What are the next three numbers in this pattern?

135, 133, 129, 121

_____, _____, _____

What are the next three numbers in this pattern?

9,600, 8,800, 8,400, 8,200

_____, _____, _____

What's next in this pattern?

Saturday
Monday
Wednesday
Friday

_____

What's next in this pattern?

March 5
March 12
March 19
March 26

_____

What's next in this pattern?

5:10
5:24
5:38
5:52

_____

Scholastic • Tic-Tac-Math: Grades 3–4

Name(s): _____

Summertime Sums

Here's an addition "warm-up" for you! Solve three addition problems to get Tic-Tac-Math!

31 + 52	43 + 16	64 + 15
500 + 300	861 + 325	746 + 170
25 45 + 22	38 74 + 59	81 76 34 + 27

Scholastic • *Tic-Tac-Math: Grades 3–4*

Name(s): _____

Addition Magician

Can you pull the answers to these problems out of your hat? Solve three addition problems to get Tic-Tac-Math!

224 + 335	576 + 521	825 + 374
6,348 + 2,557	7,284 + 4,509	5,792 + 4,319
426 209 + 647	9,084 3,275 + 8,998	7,855 679 + 2,431

Scholastic • *Tic-Tac-Math: Grades 3–4*

Name(s): _____

Addition Mysteries

Someone has stolen numbers from the equations below! Fill in the blank for three problems to get Tic-Tac-Math!

$5 +$ _____ $= 9$

$8 +$ _____ $= 15$

_____ $+ 3 = 20$

$23 +$ _____ $= 85$

_____ $+ 37 = 72$

$18 +$ _____ $= 67$

$540 +$ _____ $= 829$

$365 +$ _____ $= 1,180$

_____ $+ 2,092 = 5,275$

Name(s): _____

Estimate, Matey!

Arrr! Don't let the estimation pirate make you walk the plank. Use front-end estimation to find the sum to three problems and get Tic-Tac-Math!

ESTIMATE MATEY! ARRRR!

Estimate the sum: $3.25 + 2.19	Estimate the sum: 532 + 204	Estimate the sum: 851 + 422
Estimate the sum: $4.59 2.11 + 5.25	Estimate the sum: 654 332 + 117	Estimate the sum: 718 341 + 532
A movie ticket costs $6.25. Popcorn costs $2.95. Will $10.00 be enough to pay for a movie ticket and popcorn?	A burger costs $1.29. Fries cost $1.09. Is $3.00 enough to pay for 2 burgers and 2 fries?	On Monday, 282 people watched the school play. On Tuesday, 312 people watched it, and on Wednesday, 305 came. Did more than 800 people watch the play in all?

Scholastic • Tic-Tac-Math: Grades 3–4

Name(s): _____

The Subtraction Submarine

Prepare to dive into these subtraction problems!
Solve three problems to get Tic-Tac-Math!

172-65=107

75 − 32	58 − 28	84 − 30
63 − 18	32 − 25	91 − 54
382 − 165	438 − 254	923 − 531

Scholastic • Tic-Tac-Math: Grades 3–4

Name(s): _____

Subtraction Action

Want to earn a part in our new subtraction movie? Solve three subtraction problems to get Tic-Tac-Math!

```
  759          593          863
- 246        - 383        - 160
```

```
  302          607          503
- 116        - 239        - 345
```

```
  7,485        1,092        8,452
- 5,918      -   835      - 7,693
```

Scholastic • Tic-Tac-Math: Grades 3–4

Name(s): _____

Plus or Minus?

Should you add or subtract? You'll have to decide to solve these word problems! Solve three to get Tic-Tac-Math!

Allie earned $28 mowing lawns. Her brother Sam earned $19 mowing lawns. How much more did Allie earn than Sam?	Don ate 18 hot dogs at the hot dog–eating contest. Sal ate 6 more hot dogs than Don. How many hot dogs did Sal eat?	Juliana owns 35 comic books. Ernie owns 47 comic books. How many comic books do the two kids own in all?
Yanni weighs 134 pounds. His little sister Adelle weighs 42 pounds less. How much does Adelle weigh?	A 32-inch TV costs $749. A 27-inch TV costs $289. How much more does the 32-inch TV cost?	Olga hit a tennis ball against the wall 238 times without missing. Art hit the ball 175 times without missing. How many times did they hit the wall altogether?
Kip's family drove 1,845 miles to Dizzy World. Then they drove 2,762 miles to See World. How many miles did they drive in all?	Ginny has done 4,804 jumping jacks in gym class this year. Glenn has done 3,912. How many more jumping jacks has Ginny done?	Bart read 3,432 pages of books last year! That's 1,544 fewer pages than he read the year before. How many pages did Bart read in the two years combined?

Scholastic • *Tic-Tac-Math: Grades 3–4*

Name(s): _____

Does This Make "Cents"?

Are you savvy with money? Solve three money problems to get Tic-Tac-Math!

What is the total amount of money shown? 	What is the total amount of money shown? 	What is the total amount of money shown? 
What is the total value of one $5.00 bill, two $1.00 bills, 3 quarters, and a nickel?	What is the total value of one $10 bill, two $5.00 bills, and 6 quarters?	Say you pay for a $1.50 item with $2.00. How much change should you get back?
Say you had one $5.00 bill, two $1.00 bills, one quarter, and one dime. If you spend $2.15 cents, how much would you have left?	Say you pay for a $3.25 item with a $5.00 bill. How much change should you get back?	Say you pay for an $11.39 item with a $20.00 bill. How much change should you get back?

Name(s): _____

Tic-Tac-Times Table

How well do you know your times table?
Solve three multiplication problems to get
Tic-Tac-Math!

0 x 1 = _____	8 x 2 = _____	9 x 5 = _____
3 x 9 = _____	4 x 6 = _____	7 x 3 = _____
4 x 0 = _____	6 x 7 = _____	8 x 9 = _____

Scholastic • Tic-Tac-Math: Grades 3–4

Name(s): _____

Multiplication Mania!

Are you manic for multiplication? Solve three multiplication problems to get Tic-Tac-Math!

10 x 7 = _____

11 x 8 = _____

12 x 6 = _____

18 x 5 = _____

26 x 3 = _____

84 x 7 = _____

109 x 5 = _____

247 x 3 = _____

620 x 8 = _____

Scholastic • *Tic-Tac-Math: Grades 3–4*

Name(s): _____

Moo-ltiplication

Everyone knows cows are not good at multiplication. Are you? Solve three problems to get Tic-Tac-Math!

30 x 10	20 x 40	30 x 50
23 x 20	31 x 10	40 x 18
45 x 26	81 x 93	79 x 48

Scholastic • *Tic-Tac-Math: Grades 3–4*

Name(s): _____

Multi-Step Menu

Welcome to Benny's Burger Palace. Use the
prices on the menu board to add up each
customer's total. Solve three problems to
get Tic-Tac-Math!

Benny Burger Palace Menu

BIG Big Burger	$2.99
Baby Burger	$2.00
Chick Chick Sandwich	$2.50
Small Fries	$1.00
Super-Duper Fries	$3.00
Tiny Soda	$.50
Mega Soda	$2.49

A customer orders
4 Baby Burgers.
What is his total?

A customer orders 2
Chick Chick Sandwiches.
What is her total?

A customer orders
2 Super-Duper Fries
and 1 Tiny Soda.
What is his total?

A customer orders
2 BIG Big Burgers.
What is her total?

A customer orders
1 Chick Chick Sandwich
and 2 Mega Sodas.
What is his total?

A customer orders
2 Baby Burgers
and 2 Tiny Sodas.
What is her total?

A customer orders
2 BIG Big Burgers,
2 Baby Burgers,
1 Super-Duper Fries,
and 1 Mega Soda.
What is his total?

A customer orders
3 Baby Burgers,
2 Super-Duper Fries,
and 3 Mega Sodas.
What is her total?

A customer orders
4 BIG Big Burgers,
3 Super-Duper Fries,
and 4 Mega Sodas.
What is his total?

Scholastic • *Tic-Tac-Math: Grades 3–4*

Name(s): _____

Dive Into Division

Make a splash with division! Solve three division problems to get Tic-Tac-Math!

40 ÷ 5 = _____	36 ÷ 9 = _____	27 ÷ 3 = _____
28 ÷ 4 = _____	8 ÷ 8 = _____	0 ÷ 6 = _____
42 ÷ 6 = _____	56 ÷ 7 = _____	48 ÷ 8 = _____

Scholastic • Tic-Tac-Math: Grades 3–4

Name(s): _____

Remember the Remainder!

Solve three division problems to get
Tic-Tac-Math! Don't forget the remainder!

$2\overline{)17}$ $5\overline{)28}$ $9\overline{)50}$

$3\overline{)28}$ $4\overline{)35}$ $7\overline{)51}$

$7\overline{)67}$ $8\overline{)34}$ $10\overline{)78}$

Scholastic • Tic-Tac-Math: Grades 3–4

Name(s): _____

Cool Quotients

Who knew division could be so cool!
Solve three division problems
to get Tic-Tac-Math!

$3\overline{)63}$ $2\overline{)84}$ $9\overline{)99}$

$4\overline{)144}$ $8\overline{)656}$ $7\overline{)371}$

$4\overline{)768}$ $3\overline{)534}$ $9\overline{)828}$

Scholastic • *Tic-Tac-Math: Grades 3–4*

Name(s): _____

Fab Vocab!

Math is more than just numbers. Answer three vocabulary problems to get Tic-Tac-Math!

What is the name for the numbers being multiplied in a multiplication problem?	What is the name for the answer in a subtraction problem?	What is the name for the number that's being divided by in a division problem?
What is the name for the numbers being added in an addition problem?	What is the name for the answer in a division problem?	What is the name for the answer in an addition problem?
What is the name for what's left over in a division problem such as 12 ÷ 5?	What is the name for the answer in a multiplication problem?	What is the name for the number that's being divided in a division problem?

Name(s): _____

Times to Divide

Should you multiply or divide? Find out when you solve three word problems to get Tic-Tac-Math!

Three friends split a $15 meal. If each pays the same amount, how much does each friend owe?	Alex, Manny, Derek, and Barry each owns 8 baseball cards. How many cards do they have in all?	Pop buys 9 packs of gum with 5 sticks of gum in each pack. How many sticks of gum does Pop have in all?
Annie has 84 stickers. She keeps an equal number of stickers on each of 7 pages in her sticker book. How many stickers are on each page?	Barry spent 17 minutes on his writing homework. He spent 3 times as long on his math homework. How long did Barry spend on math homework?	There are 72 cookies in a box. Inside the box are 3 wrapped sleeves, each with an equal number of cookies in it. How many cookies are in each sleeve?
Britt is saving up to buy a $252 video-game system. If she saves $6 per week, how long will she need to save?	Conrad is counting down hours until his birthday, which is exactly 21 days from now. There are 24 hours in a day. How many hours away is Conrad's birthday?	If a car could drive 54 miles per hour for 218 hours, how far could it travel?

Scholastic • *Tic-Tac-Math: Grades 3–4*

Name(s): _____

It's Too Much!

Dig up only the information you need to solve these problems. Solve three problems to get Tic-Tac-Math!

At 6:00 P.M., Johnny bought a calculator for $4.95 and a protractor for $1.80. How much did Johnny spend in all?

During their fishing trip, Patty caught 5 fish. One of them weighed 15 pounds! Patty's sister caught twice as many fish. How many fish did Patty's sister catch?

There are 27 kids in Anabeth's class, 26 kids in Carlos's class, and 24 kids in Pete's class. How many more kids are in Carlos's class than in Pete's class?

Andrea's basketball team won their game 54 to 48. Andrea and Gail scored 24 of the team's points! If Gail scored 10 points, how many points did Andrea score?

Drake spent 28 minutes on 20 math problems, and 30 minutes writing 5 essays. How much longer did he spend on the essays than on the math problems?

A movie ticket costs 2 times as much as popcorn, and 3 times as much as a soda. If a movie costs $9.00, how much is popcorn?

In a football game, Dale scored 3 touchdowns and Jimmy scored 4. If a touchdown is worth 6 points, how many points did Jimmy score?

There are 15,000 people in Bigville. That's 2,000 more than are in Middleville, and 5,000 more than are in Littleville. How many people live in Littleville?

A 6-bedroom house in Homesburg costs $250,000 and a 4-bedroom house costs half as much. How much is a 4-bedroom house in Homesburg?

Name(s): _____

Name That Fraction!

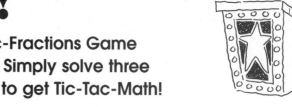

It's time to play the Tic-Tac-Fractions Game Show that everyone loves. Simply solve three fraction-naming problems to get Tic-Tac-Math!

What fraction of this shape is shaded? 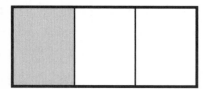	What fraction of this set is shaded? 	What fraction of these numbers is even? 1 6 3 7 4 9 5
Matt has 4 red balloons, 3 green ones, and 2 yellow ones. What fraction of his balloons is red?	Lilly has 6 pairs of white socks, 4 pairs of yellow ones, and 3 pairs of red socks. What fraction of her pairs of socks is yellow?	Jacob has 5 quarters, 7 dimes, 3 nickels, and 2 pennies. What fraction of his coins are dimes?
About what fraction of this pie is left? a. $\frac{2}{3}$ b. $\frac{1}{3}$ 	About what fraction of this cake is left? a. $\frac{1}{4}$ b. $\frac{1}{2}$ 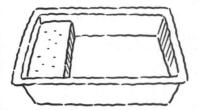	About what fraction of this jar is full? a. $\frac{1}{2}$ b. $\frac{5}{6}$ 

Name(s): _____

I'm $\frac{1}{2}$, But Call Me $\frac{2}{4}$

What's in a name? Well, if you're a fraction, you could have lots of names. Find out more when you solve three equivalent fraction problems to get Tic-Tac-Math!

$\frac{1}{2} = \frac{?}{4}$

$\frac{2}{3} = \frac{?}{6}$

$\frac{3}{12} = \frac{?}{8}$

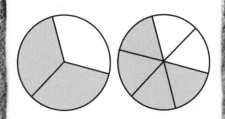

Are the fractions shown equivalent?

Are the fractions shown equivalent?

Are the fractions shown equivalent?

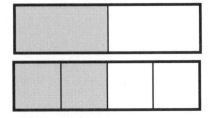

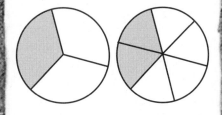

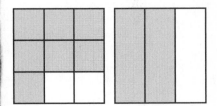

Which of these fractions is equivalent to $\frac{2}{3}$?

$\frac{4}{5}$ $\frac{8}{12}$ $\frac{6}{8}$

Which of these fractions is equivalent to $\frac{5}{9}$?

$\frac{45}{81}$ $\frac{25}{29}$

$\frac{48}{63}$ $\frac{20}{35}$

Which of these fractions is equivalent to $\frac{12}{16}$?

$\frac{36}{40}$ $\frac{2}{9}$ $\frac{48}{54}$

$\frac{6}{8}$ $\frac{20}{25}$

Scholastic • Tic-Tac-Math: Grades 3–4

Name(s): _____

Fractions Made Simplest

Fractions don't have to be so hard. In fact, they prefer to be simple. Solve three simplifying fraction problems to get Tic-Tac-Math!

What is the greatest common factor of 6 and 8?	What is the greatest common factor of 4 and 12?	What is the greatest common factor of 15 and 25?
What is $\frac{6}{8}$ in simplest form?	What is $\frac{4}{12}$ in simplest form?	What is $\frac{15}{25}$ in simplest form?
What is $\frac{4}{18}$ in simplest form?	What is $\frac{12}{42}$ in simplest form?	What is $\frac{30}{75}$ in simplest form?

Name(s): _____

Out of Order

We're sorry, but this activity is out of order.
Solve three ordering fraction problems
to get Tic-Tac-Math!

Fill in the box with
>, <, or =.

$$\frac{2}{8} \quad \square \quad \frac{5}{8}$$

Fill in the box with
>, <, or =.

$$\frac{2}{10} \quad \square \quad \frac{1}{5}$$

Fill in the box with
>, <, or =.

$$\frac{1}{2} \quad \square \quad \frac{1}{4}$$

Fill in the box with
>, <, or =.

$$\frac{3}{4} \quad \square \quad \frac{9}{12}$$

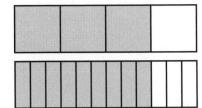

Fill in the box with
>, <, or =.

$$\frac{5}{6} \quad \square \quad \frac{7}{8}$$

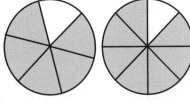

Fill in the box with
>, <, or =.

$$\frac{8}{10} \quad \square \quad \frac{4}{6}$$

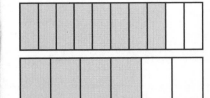

Order these fractions
from greatest to least:

$$\frac{1}{6} \quad \frac{2}{3} \quad \frac{1}{3}$$

Order these fractions
from greatest to least:

$$\frac{5}{8} \quad \frac{3}{4} \quad \frac{1}{4} \quad \frac{3}{8}$$

Order these fractions
from greatest to least:

$$\frac{3}{4} \quad \frac{5}{6} \quad \frac{7}{12} \quad \frac{2}{3}$$

Name(s): _____

Fractions in Action!

Be a fraction hero: Solve three fraction problems to get Tic-Tac-Math!

Use the counters shown to find $\frac{1}{4}$ of 20. ○	Use the counters shown to find $\frac{2}{3}$ of 18. ○ ○ ○ ○ ○ ○ ○ ○ ○ ○ ○ ○ ○ ○ ○ ○ ○ ○	Use the counters shown to find $\frac{5}{7}$ of 28. ○
What is $\frac{1}{2}$ of 30?	What is $\frac{3}{5}$ of 15?	What is $\frac{5}{8}$ of 32?
Julie had 24 N&N's candies. She gave $\frac{1}{4}$ of them to her brother Gary. How many candies did she give to Gary?	Andrew saw his grandmother on $\frac{2}{7}$ of the days in the past two weeks. (Two weeks is 14 days.) How many days did Andrew see his grandmother?	Rachel and Gregory played 36 games of chess. Rachel won $\frac{5}{9}$ of the games. How many games did Rachel win?

Scholastic • Tic-Tac-Math: Grades 3–4

Name(s): _____

Mix-Ups in the Kitchen

Don't get mixed up by mixed numbers in the kitchen! Solve three problems to get Tic-Tac-Math!

Write a mixed number that expresses how much of the pizzas are left.

| Write a mixed number that expresses how much of the soda six-packs is left.

| Shade the diagram to show $2\frac{3}{4}$.

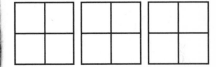

Shade the diagram to show $3\frac{1}{6}$.

| Lucille cut 2 pies into 6 slices each. If Lucille's family eats $1\frac{5}{6}$ pies, how many slices were eaten?

| Express $\frac{8}{5}$ as a mixed number.

Express $\frac{7}{3}$ as a mixed number.

| Express $2\frac{1}{2}$ as an improper fraction.

| Antoine is making cookies. His recipe calls for 2 cups of sugar. He has $\frac{17}{8}$ cups of sugar. Does he have enough?

Name(s): _____

Some Fraction Sums

Find the sum or difference of each set of fractions. Solve three problems to get Tic-Tac-Math!

$\dfrac{2}{4} + \dfrac{1}{4} =$	$\dfrac{5}{6} - \dfrac{4}{6} =$	Mona got 9 out of 10 questions correct on a quiz. What fraction of the questions did she answer incorrectly?
Add and simplify. $\dfrac{3}{8} + \dfrac{3}{8} =$	Subtract and simplify. $\dfrac{7}{10} - \dfrac{2}{10} =$	Jack's new CD has 14 songs on it. He loves $\dfrac{5}{14}$ of its songs and really likes another $\dfrac{2}{14}$ of them. What fraction of the songs does Jack love or really like?
$\dfrac{1}{2} + \dfrac{1}{4} =$	$\dfrac{5}{12} - \dfrac{1}{6} =$	Lucy spent $\dfrac{9}{20}$ of her birthday money on sporting goods and $\dfrac{3}{10}$ of it on DVDs. What fraction of her birthday money did she spend in all?

Name(s): _____

Crazy About Decimals!

You may not love decimals as much as this kid does. But you'll get to like them when you solve three problems and get Tic-Tac-Math!

Name the shaded part as a decimal:

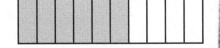

Name the shaded part as a decimal:

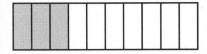

Name the shaded part as a decimal:

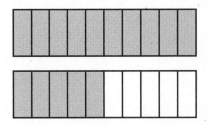

Name the shaded part as a decimal:

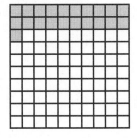

Name the shaded part as a decimal:

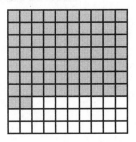

Name the shaded part as a decimal:

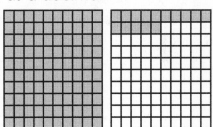

Put these decimals in order from least to greatest:

5.65
5.56
5.6
5.5

Put these decimals in order from least to greatest:

10.34
10.43
10.04
10.4
10.3
10.14

Put these decimals in order from least to greatest:

4.85
4.58
4.9
4.8
4.81
4.5

Name(s): _____

Decimal Round-Up

Giddyap! Solve three decimal and fraction problems to get Tic-Tac-Math!

Use the number line to round 3.79 to the nearest whole number.

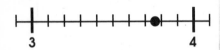

3   4

Use the number line to round 1.27 to the nearest whole number.

1   2

Use the number line to round 5.54 to the nearest whole number.

5   6

Round 7.38 to the nearest whole number.

Ivana took 2.43 seconds to answer a test question. Is that closer to 2 minutes or 3 minutes?

Glenn gulped down his sandwich in 4.61 minutes. Is that closer to 4 minutes or 5 minutes?

What is the decimal equivalent of $\frac{3}{20}$?

What is the decimal equivalent of $\frac{4}{5}$?

Jan spent $\frac{7}{10}$ of a dollar on a newspaper. Write that amount as a decimal value in cents.

Scholastic • Tic-Tac-Math: Grades 3–4

Name(s): _____

Pointy Decimal Points!

Watch out for the pointy porcupine! See how sharp your decimal addition and subtraction skills are by solving three problems to get Tic-Tac-Math!

3.2 + 4.1 = _____	5.8 + 2.6 = _____	7.3 – 6.9 = _____
$2.45 + 1.38 ———	5.53 – 3.72 ———	4.5 + 6.75 ———
7.63 – 3.8 ———	1.87 9.29 + 3.48 ———	6.8 6.54 6.88 + 7.01 ———

Name(s): _____

The Last Word on Fractions and Decimals

Answer three questions to get Tic-Tac-Math!

What is the name for the value on the top of a fraction?	What is the name for the value on the bottom of a fraction?	What is the name for a fraction that has 1 as its numerator?
What is the place value of the 1 in 5.21?	What is the place value of the 7 in 9.73?	Which decimal has an 8 in its tenths place? 82.45 24.85 24.58 28.54
Which fraction has a denominator of 5? $\frac{3}{5}$ $\frac{5}{8}$ $5\frac{1}{3}$	What is the name for a fraction where the numerator is greater than its denominator?	Which fraction is in simplest form? $\frac{4}{10}$ $\frac{3}{9}$ $\frac{7}{15}$ $\frac{8}{22}$

Scholastic • Tic-Tac-Math: Grades 3–4

Name(s): _____

Tic-TOCK Math!

You're right on time to solve three
problems and get Tic-Tac-Math!

Write the time
shown here
two different
ways.

_____

_____

Write the time
shown here
two different
ways.

_____

_____

Write the time
shown here
two different
ways.

_____

_____

Write the time
shown here
two different
ways.

_____

_____

Write the time
shown here
two different
ways.

_____

_____

Write the time
shown here
two different
ways.

_____

_____

Draw hands on the clock
to show half past seven.

Draw hands on the clock
to show 3:19.

Draw hands on the clock to
show a quarter to twelve.

Scholastic • Tic-Tac-Math: Grades 3–4

Name(s): _____

Time for School!

Anita is keeping track of time during a school day. Take a few minutes to solve three problems and get Tic-Tac-Math!

Anita wakes up at 6:00 A.M. She lays in bed for another 15 minutes. At what time does she get up?

Anita eats breakfast from 7:00 A.M. until 7:22 A.M. For how long does she eat breakfast?

One day, Anita missed the bus and got to school at 8:18 A.M. But school started at 8:00 A.M.! How late was Anita?

Anita's first class starts at 8:00 A.M. It is a double-math class that lasts 1 hour and 35 minutes. At what time does math class end?

Anita's gym class runs from 10:30 A.M. until 11:15 A.M. How long is gym class?

Anita's whole school day lasts from 8:00 A.M. to 2:30 P.M. How long is that?

Yesterday afternoon, Anita played soccer after school from 2:45 P.M. until 4:12 P.M. For how long did she play?

One day, a school assembly ran from 9:40 A.M. until 12:05 P.M. How long was the assembly?

After a busy school day, Anita was so tired, she slept from 6:52 P.M. until 5:40 A.M. For how long did Anita sleep?

Scholastic • *Tic-Tac-Math: Grades 3–4*

Name(s): _____

Temperature Is Cool!

**Are you cool enough to get Tic-Tac-Math?
Solve three temperature problems and see!**

What temperature does this thermometer read in degrees Fahrenheit?

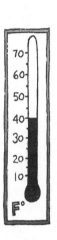

What temperature does this thermometer read in degrees Celsius?

What temperature does this thermometer read in degrees Fahrenheit?

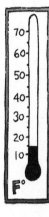

What is the equivalent of 32 degrees Fahrenheit in degrees Celsius?

Which is warmer: 50°F or 50°C?

Which is warmer: 10°F or 10°C?

How many degrees colder is 25°C than 42°C?

How many degrees colder is –3°C than 5°C?

How many degrees colder is –15°C than 17°C?

Name(s): _____

Amazing Feet–and Inches

**It shouldn't take you "long" to get Tic-Tac-Math!
Just solve three measurement problems.**

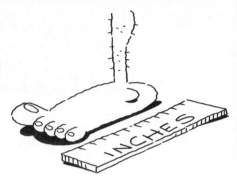

4 feet = _____ inches	5 feet = _____ inches	3 feet, 2 inches = _____ inches
2 yards = _____ feet	4 yards, 2 feet = _____ feet	1 mile = _____ feet
2 miles = _____ yards	1 mile, 300 feet = _____ feet	Frank ran 2,100 yards from school to home in 7 minutes. How would you express that distance in miles and feet?

Scholastic • *Tic-Tac-Math: Grades 3–4*

Name(s): _____

Shape Up!

Name three of the two- and three-dimensional shapes to get Tic-Tac-Math!

Name(s): _____

All Kinds of Lines

You're not just getting a line here.
Solve three problems to get Tic-Tac-Math!

Is this a line, a ray, or a line segment?

Is this a line, a ray, or a line segment?

Is this a line, a ray, or a line segment?

Are the lines intersecting or parallel?

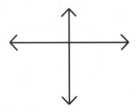

Are the lines intersecting or parallel?

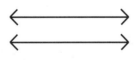

Are the lines intersecting or parallel?

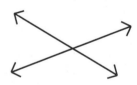

Are the lines parallel or perpendicular?

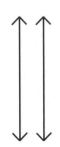

Are the lines parallel or perpendicular?

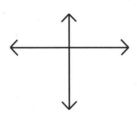

Are the lines parallel or perpendicular?

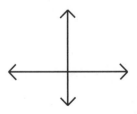

Name(s): _____

The Bermuda Right Angle

There's no mystery to this activity. Just solve three angle and polygon problems to get Tic-Tac-Math!

Is this angle greater than, less than, or equal to a right angle? 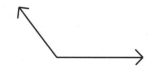	Is this angle greater than, less than, or equal to a right angle? 	Is this angle greater than, less than, or equal to a right angle? 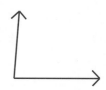
Is this an acute, obtuse, or right angle? 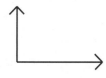	Is this an acute, obtuse, or right angle? 	Is this an acute, obtuse, or right angle? 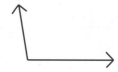
Is this triangle acute, obtuse, or right? 	Is this triangle acute, obtuse, or right? 	Is this triangle acute, obtuse, or right? 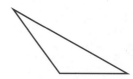

Scholastic • Tic-Tac-Math: Grades 3–4

Name(s): _____

Four-Sided Shapes

A quadrilateral can be a parallelogram, square, rectangle, rhombus, or trapezoid. Name three quadrilaterals to get Tic-Tac-Math! Try to use the most precise name as possible.

Scholastic • *Tic-Tac-Math: Grades 3–4*

Name(s): _____

The Symmetry Tree

We found all of these objects up in the branches of our symmetry tree! Draw any lines of symmetry on three diagrams to get Tic-Tac-Math!

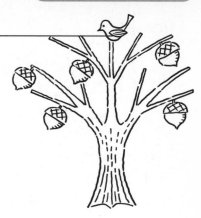

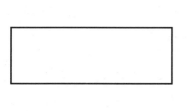

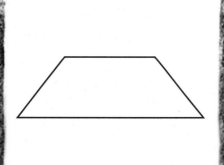
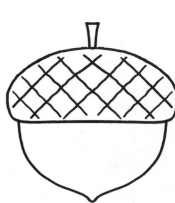
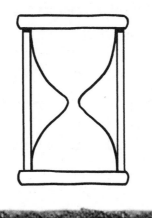
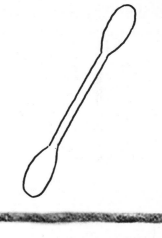

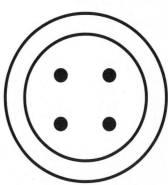

Scholastic • Tic-Tac-Math: Grades 3–4

Name(s): _____

Playground Perimeters

Some playground equipment and sandboxes look like the shapes below. Solve three perimeter problems to get Tic-Tac-Math!

What is the perimeter of this triangle?

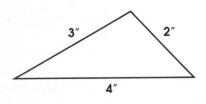

3″ 2″
4″

What is the perimeter of this rectangle?

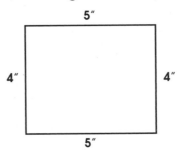

5″
4″   4″
5″

What is the perimeter of this shape?

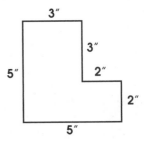

3″
3″
5″   2″
2″
5″

What is this shape's perimeter?

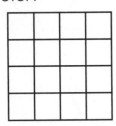

What is this shape's perimeter?

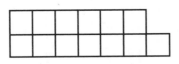

What is this shape's perimeter?

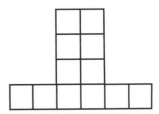

What is this shape's perimeter?

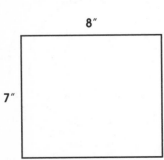

8″
7″

What is this shape's perimeter?

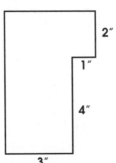

2″
1″
4″
3″

What is this shape's perimeter?

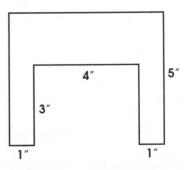

4″   5″
3″
1″   1″

Name(s): _____

Area Has Got You Covered

How many square feet of wallpaper do you need to cover these walls? Learn about area when you solve three problems and get Tic-Tac-Math!

What is the area of this shape?

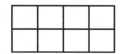

What is the area of this shape?

What is the area of this shape?

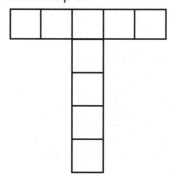

What is the area of this shape?

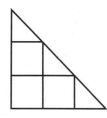

What is the area of this shape?

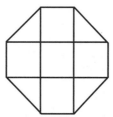

What is the area of this rectangle?

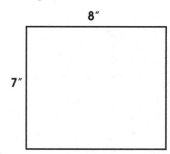

8″

7″

What is the area of this shape?

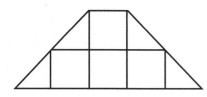

What is the area of this rectangle?

12″

9″

What is the area of this rectangle?

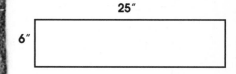

25″

6″

Scholastic • *Tic-Tac-Math: Grades 3–4*

Name(s): _____

Fill in the Volume

Volume is not just about sound—it's also about how many cubic units can fit inside a shape. Solve three volume problems to get Tic-Tac-Math!

What is the volume of this shape? 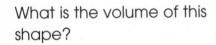 	What is the volume of this shape? 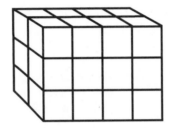	What is the volume of this shape? 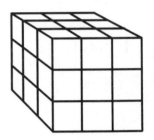
What is the volume of this shape? 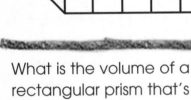	What is the volume of this shape? 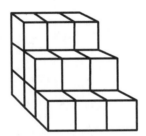	What is the volume of this shape? 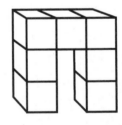
What is the volume of a rectangular prism that's 3 inches by 2 inches by 6 inches?	What is the volume of a rectangular prism that's 8 inches by 4 inches by 9 inches?	What is the volume of a cube that has sides of 7 inches?

Scholastic • *Tic-Tac-Math: Grades 3–4*

Name(s): _____

Kid on a Grid

Jamaal just moved to a new town. This map shows the street corners where different places are located. Help Jamaal find his way around! Solve three coordinate-grid problems to get Tic-Tac-Math!

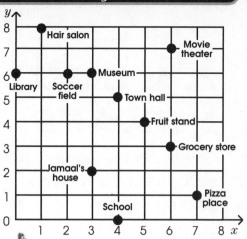

What is directly above the school on the map?	What is located at (2, 6)?	What is located at (5, 4)?
What are the coordinates of the hair salon?	What are the coordinates of the pizza place?	Which place has the same x-coordinate as the movie theater?
Jamaal rides his bike on the roads from the school to the library at a rate of one block per minute. If he stays on the roads on the grid and he doesn't backtrack, how long will the trip take him?	Jamaal's bike gets a flat tire, so he walks it home from the library. If he walks one block every five minutes and stays on the roads without back-tracking, how long will the walk take?	How many different routes could Jamaal take on the roads from the museum to the fruit stand without backtracking?

53

Name(s): _____

X's and Pict-O's

Check out this "sweet" pictograph. Solve three problems to get Tic-Tac-Math!

Favorite Candies of Students in Mrs. Coco's Fourth-Grade Class

Snackers Bars: 0 0 0 0

Gunky Way Bars: 0 0

Dummi Bears: 0 0 (

Key: 0 = 4 students

What does each 0 on the graph stand for?	Which candy did most students choose as their favorite?	Which candy did the fewest students pick as their favorite?
How many students chose Snackers Bars as their favorite candy?	How many students chose Gunky Way as their favorite candy?	What does each (on the graph stand for?
How many students chose Dummi Bears as their favorite candy?	How many more students chose Dummi Bears as their favorite than chose Gunky Way bars?	How many more students chose Snackers Bars as their favorite than chose Dummi Bears?

Name(s): _____

One Wild Bar Graph!

See how fast you can solve the problems on this grid. Solve three to get Tic-Tac-Math!

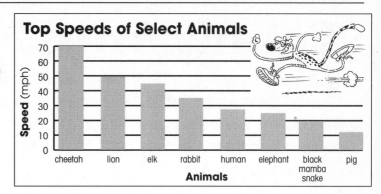

Top Speeds of Select Animals

(Speed (mph) — 70, 60, 50, 40, 30, 20, 10, 0; Animals: cheetah, lion, elk, rabbit, human, elephant, black mamba snake, pig)

What does each bar on the graph show?	Which animal on the graph moves the fastest?	Which animal on the graph moves the slowest?
What is the fastest an elephant can move?	What is the fastest a rabbit can move?	Which animal has a top speed of 45 mph?
About how much faster is a black mamba snake than a pig?	About how much slower is a human than a cheetah?	Which animal is about twice as fast as an elephant?

Name(s): _____

Totally Snowy!

How much snow did the town of Blizzardville get this past winter? Read this line graph to find out. You should have "snow" problem solving three problems to get Tic-Tac-Math!

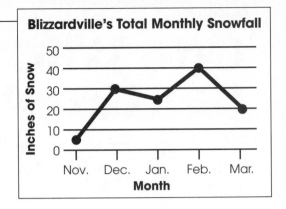

Blizzardville's Total Monthly Snowfall

In which month was there the greatest amount of snowfall?

Did the total snowfall increase or decrease between December and January?

How many inches of snow fell in March?

How many inches of snow fell in February?

How many inches of snow fell in November?

Do you think the amount of snowfall increased, decreased, or stayed the same between March and April?

How much less snow was there in November than there was in March?

In which month was there about twice as much snow as there was in March?

In which month was there about 10 inches less snowfall than there was in December?

Name(s): _____

Above-Average Players

Check out these statistics and prices. Find the average of the numbers in each square. Solve three problems to get Tic-Tac-Math!

Lacin' Williams
Game 1: 8 assists
Game 2: 5 assists
Game 3: 5 assists

Jordan Michael
Game 1: 7 rebounds
Game 2: 4 rebounds
Game 3: 9 rebounds
Game 4: 12 rebounds

Shanille O'Keel
Game 1: 9 free throws
Game 2: 3 free throws
Game 3: 4 free throws
Game 4: 0 free throws

Chasey McGravy
Game 1: 28 points
Game 2: 35 points
Game 3: 29 points
Game 4: 28 points

LeMon Fames
Game 1: 38 points
Game 2: 31 points
Game 3: 27 points
Game 4: 33 points
Game 5: 41 points

Slam Duncan
Game 1: 22 points
Game 2: 19 points
Game 3: 25 points
Game 4: 26 points
Game 5: 28 points

Price of a soda at different basketball stadiums:
Stadium 1: $2.50
Stadium 2: $4.00
Stadium 3: $2.50

Price of a hot dog at different basketball stadiums:
Stadium 1: $4.50
Stadium 2: $4.75
Stadium 3: $3.50

Value of Jordan Michael's autograph:
1989: $3.25
1994: $5.85
1999: $7.45
2004: $9.85

Name(s): _____

What's Your Probability Ability?

What are your chances of winning this game?
It depends on how well you understand probability!
Solve three problems to get Tic-Tac-Math!

Sue has 5 blue shirts and 3 red ones. If she picks a shirt at random, is she more likely to pick a blue shirt or a red one?

If Babs picks up a block at random, what letter does she have the better chance of grabbing?

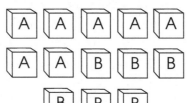

If Penny picks one coin at random, which type of coin does she have the best chance of picking?

What pattern do you have the greatest chance of spinning?

What pattern do you have the greatest chance of spinning?

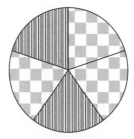

What pattern do you have the greatest chance of spinning?

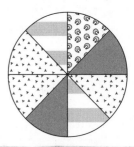

Express the chances of spinning zigzags as a fraction.

Express the chances of spinning polka dots as a fraction.

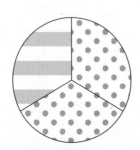

Express the chances of spinning x's as a fraction.

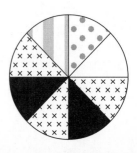

Scholastic • Tic-Tac-Math: Grades 3–4

Answers

Order in the Court!
(p. 9)

<	>	>
=	>	<

4,582	30,458	560,987
5,725	31,008	567,089
5,820	31,201	567,098
5,872	32,000	567,890
	38,562	567,980

The Rounding Hound
(p. 10)

80	40	70
400	300	700
5,000	90,000	35,580

Do You See a Pattern?
(p. 11)

10 (add 2 to the previous number)	13 (add 3 to the previous number)	25 (subtract 5 from the previous number)
25, 24, 27 (add 3 to the previous number; subtract 1 from the total)	105, 73, 9 (subtract 2, then 4, then 8, then 16, and so on; the number subtracted from each number is 2 times the number that was subtracted from the previous number)	8,100, 8,050, 8,025 (subtract 800, then 400, then 200, and so on; the number subtracted from each number is $\frac{1}{2}$ the number subtracted from the previous number)
Sunday (add 2 days to the previous day of the week)	April 2 (add 1 week to the previous date)	6:06 (add 14 minutes to the previous time)

Summertime Sums
(p. 12)

83	59	79
800	1,186	916
92	171	218

Addition Magician
(p. 13)

559	1,097	1,199
8,905	11,793	10,111
1,282	21,357	10,965

Addition Mysteries
(p. 14)

4	7	17
62	35	49
289	815	3,183

Estimate, Matey!
(p. 15)

$5.00	700	1,200
$11.00	1,000	1,500
yes	no	yes

The Subtraction Submarine
(p. 16)

43	30	54
45	7	37
217	184	392

Subtraction Action
(p. 17)

513	210	703
186	368	158
1,567	257	759

Plus or Minus?
(p. 18)

$9 more	24 hot dogs	82 comic books
92 pounds	$460 more	413 times
4,607 miles	892 more jumping jacks	8,408 pages

Does This Make "Cents"?
(p. 19)

$.48	$.76	$1.07
$7.80	$21.50	$.50
$5.20	$1.75	$8.61

Tic-Tac-Times Table
(p. 20)

0	16	45
27	24	21
0	42	72

Multiplication Mania!
(p. 21)

70	88	72
90	78	588
545	741	4,960

Moo-ltiplication
(p. 22)

300	800	1,500
460	310	720
1,170	7,533	3,792

Multi-Step Menu
(p. 23)

$8.00	$5.00	$6.50
$5.98	$7.48	$5.00
$15.47	$19.47	$30.92

Dive Into Division
(p. 24)

8	4	9
7	1	0
7	8	6

Remember the Remainder!
(p. 25)

8 R1	5 R3	5 R5
9 R1	8 R3	7 R2
9 R4	4 R2	7 R8

Cool Quotients
(p. 26)

21	42	11
36	82	53
192	178	92

Fab Vocab!
(p. 27)

factors	difference	divisor
addends	quotient	sum
remainder	product	dividend

Times to Divide
(p. 28)

$5 each	32 baseball cards	45 sticks of gum
12 stickers	51 minutes	24 cookies
42 weeks	504 hours	11,772 miles

It's Too Much!
(p. 29)

$6.75	10 fish	2 more kids
14 points	2 minutes longer	$4.50
24 points	10,000 people	$125,000

Name That Fraction!
(p. 30)

$\frac{1}{3}$	$\frac{3}{5}$	$\frac{2}{7}$
$\frac{4}{9}$	$\frac{4}{13}$	$\frac{7}{17}$
b	a	a

I'm $\frac{1}{2}$, But Call Me $\frac{2}{4}$
(p. 31)

2	4	2
no	yes	no
$\frac{8}{12}$	$\frac{45}{81}$	$\frac{6}{8}$

Fractions Made Simplest
(p. 32)

2	4	5
$\frac{3}{4}$	$\frac{1}{3}$	$\frac{3}{5}$
$\frac{2}{9}$	$\frac{2}{7}$	$\frac{2}{5}$

Out of Order
(p. 33)

<	=	>
=	<	>
$\frac{2}{3}$, $\frac{1}{3}$, $\frac{1}{6}$	$\frac{3}{4}$, $\frac{5}{8}$, $\frac{3}{8}$, $\frac{1}{4}$	$\frac{5}{6}$, $\frac{3}{4}$, $\frac{2}{3}$, $\frac{7}{12}$

Fractions in Action!
(p. 34)

5	12	20
15	9	20
6 N&N's	4 days	20 games

Mix-ups in the Kitchen
(p. 35)

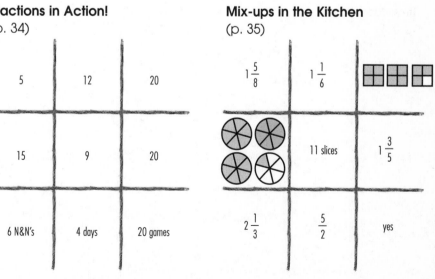

$1\frac{5}{8}$	$1\frac{1}{6}$	
	11 slices	$1\frac{3}{5}$
$2\frac{1}{3}$	$\frac{5}{2}$	yes

Some Fraction Sums
(p. 36)

$\frac{3}{4}$	$\frac{1}{6}$	$\frac{1}{10}$
$\frac{3}{4}$	$\frac{1}{2}$	$\frac{1}{2}$ of the songs
$\frac{3}{4}$	$\frac{1}{4}$	$\frac{3}{4}$ of her birthday money

Crazy About Decimals!
(p. 37)

0.6	0.3	1.5
0.21	0.72	1.15
5.5, 5.56, 5.6, 5.65	10.04, 10.14, 10.3, 10.34, 10.4, 10.43	4.5, 4.58, 4.8, 4.81, 4.85, 4.9

Decimal Round-Up
(p. 38)

4	1	6
7	2 minutes	5 minutes
0.15	0.8	$.70

Pointy Decimals Points!
(p. 39)

7.3	8.4	0.4
$3.83	1.81	11.25
3.83	14.64	27.23

The Last Word on Fractions and Decimals (p. 40)

numerator	denominator	unit fraction
hundredths	tenths	24.85
$\frac{3}{5}$	improper fraction	$\frac{7}{15}$

Tic-TOCK Math!
(p. 41)

6:05, six o five, 5 after 6, five minutes after six	7:50, 10 to 8, seven-fifty, 50 after 7	8:55, eight fifty-five, 5 of 9, five minutes to nine
4:27, four twenty-seven, 27 after 4, twenty-seven minutes after four	12:13, twelve thirteen, 13 after 12, thirteen minutes after twelve	1:45, one forty-five, a quarter to 2, fifteen minutes to two

Time for School!
(p. 42)

6:15 A.M.	22 minutes	18 minutes late
9:35 A.M.	45 minutes (:45)	6 hours, 30 minutes (6:30)
1 hour, 27 minutes (1:27)	2 hours, 25 minutes (2:25)	11 hours, 48 minutes (11:48)

Temperature Is Cool!
(p. 43)

40°F	7°C	15°F
0°C	50°C	10°C
17°C colder	8°C colder	32°C colder

Amazing Feet—and Inches
(p. 44)

48	60	38
6	14	5,280
3,520	5,580	1 mile, 1,020 feet

Shape Up!
(p. 45)

rectangle	circle	triangle
pyramid	sphere	rectangular prism
hexagon	octagon	pentagon

All Kinds of Lines
(p. 46)

ray	line segment	line
intersecting	parallel	intersecting
parallel	perpendicular	perpendicular

The Bermuda Right Angle
(p. 47)

greater than	less than	less than
right angle	acute angle	obtuse angle
acute triangle	right triangle	obtuse triangle

Four-Sided Shapes
(p. 48)

square	rectangle	rectangle
quadrilateral	parallelogram	trapezoid
rhombus	trapezoid	parallelogram

The Symmetry Tree
(p. 49)

no lines of symmetry		

Playground Perimeters
(p. 50)

9"	18"	20"
16 units	18 units	20 units
30"	20"	28"

Area Has Got You Covered
(p. 51)

8 square units	4 square units	9 square units
4.5 square units	7 square units	56 square inches
6 square units	108 square inches	150 square inches

Fill in the Volume
(p. 52)

4 cubic units	24 cubic units	27 cubic units
35 cubic units	18 cubic units	7 cubic units
36 cubic inches	288 cubic inches	343 cubic inches

Kid on a Grid
(p. 53)

town hall	soccer field	fruit stand
(1, 8)	(7, 1)	grocery store
10 minutes	35 minutes	6 routes

X's and Pict-O's
(p. 54)

4 students	Snackers Bars	Gunky Way Bars
16 students	8 students	2 students
10 students	2 more students	6 more students

One Wild Bar Graph!
(p. 55)

the speed of each animal in miles per hour	cheetah	pig
25 mph	35 mph	elk
about 10 mph faster	about 40 mph slower	lion

Totally Snowy!
(p. 56)

February	decrease	20 inches
40 inches	5 inches	decreased
15 inches less	February	March

Above-Average Players
(p. 57)

6 assists	8 rebounds	4 free throws
30 points	34 points	24 points
$3.00	$4.25	$6.60

What's Your Probability Ability?
(p. 58)

blue shirt	letter "A"	nickel
$\frac{1}{6}$	$\frac{2}{3}$	$\frac{3}{8}$